CHRIS BRUNNEN
Portsmouth Area

Including Havant, Gosport, Fareham & Waterlooville

With Contributions by Jim Bramble

On our aerial tour, we will be flying in a helicopter at around 1,000ft, to take a look at many of the towns and villages in the Portsmouth area as well as flying over the city itself. We'll see how the landscape has changed over the last 65 years to accommodate the ever-growing population.

In memory of Andrew Biddlecombe
1950-2020

My first ever aerial photographic flight – to photograph IBM in Havant – was
commissioned by Andrew, of Tandem Advertising, in 1987.

Sadly, he passed away just as this book was going to print but some
of the photographs from that flight are in this book.

Printed in England
ISBN: 978-1-8380819-0-4

Jim and I meet up at our old school, The City of Portsmouth Technical High School,
now Trafalgar Academy.

Photo credit: Habib Shipu Rahman. The News, Portsmouth.

Pre-flight briefing

My interest in photography was triggered by my best friend and neighbour at the time, Neil Morris. He came home from school one day in the early 1970s and showed me what he had done that day. He passed me an envelope over the garden fence and I pulled out some black and white photographs. I couldn't believe this was something that could be done by kids at school and wanted to know all about it.

At the first opportunity I took up the option to study photography in art lessons at my school, The Technical High School, and was able to use their 35mm cameras and equipment. I learned how to develop film and print photographs for myself, studied the practical, theoretical and historical aspects of the subject, and earned 'O' and 'A' level photography qualifications. I also studied art, technical drawing, physics and chemistry – all essential subjects in the art and science of photography. This is also how I was to meet Mr Bramble, as he was my technical drawing teacher. Looking back now I can clearly remember seeing numerous rolls of film hanging up to dry in a converted storeroom-come-darkroom he had at the back of the classroom.

After leaving school I studied graphic design at Portsmouth College of Art but found myself spending most of my time in the studios and darkrooms of the photography department. After leaving college I worked for five years at a small photography and design studio producing brochures and corporate advertising material, where I photographed products in the studio one day, and designed a brochure for them the next. Some changes in the firm prompted me to start my own business and, with their help, I started trading as CJB Photography in 1986. The following year I was commissioned by a regular client to take some aerial photographs of a site in Havant. This was to be the first of many aerial photography flights in my professional career.

It was many years later that I came across a website with a gallery of old aerial photographs that were credited to someone named Jim Bramble, who turned out to be the same Jim Bramble from my school days! Looking through this on-line archive I soon realised that we had taken some very similar photographs, just many years apart, and the idea of putting something together to compare our 'old' and new photographs was born. I managed to get in touch with the now 91-year-old Jim, who was delighted with my idea and that his old photographs could be put to use. Shortly after, a CD containing his photographs arrived, but it came with the news that in the years since these scans were made, Jim had moved house to 'downsize', and in the process all his original negatives, prints and slides had, sadly, been lost. All that survived were the scanned versions on this disc.

It appears that both Jim and I share a passion for photography and flying and I find it quite extraordinary that those films I saw hanging up to dry all those years ago may well have been some of the photographs on that website and that you can now see in this book.

Navigator

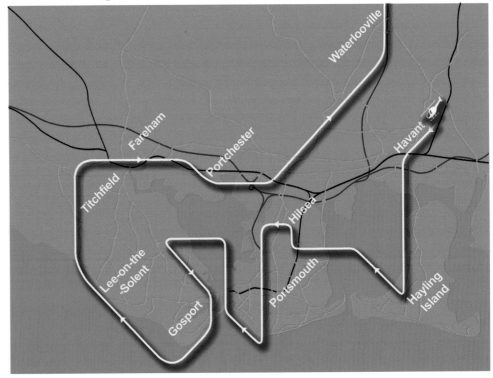

Starting at Havant, we go to Langstone and Hayling Island, then across Langstone Harbour to travel the length of Portsea Island from Hilsea to Southsea. We then go up Portsmouth Harbour to see the dockyard and commercial port before crossing over Portsmouth Harbour to Hardway. Now we head south to Gosport and Haslar before turning west to Lee-on-the-Solent. At this point, we head inland to Titchfield, Fareham, over to Portchester, then to Cosham before heading north to Widley and Waterlooville, as far as Horndean.

Flight Information

The majority of Jim's surviving photographs were of Portsmouth so my first book, *Portsmouth; an Aerial Tour Through Time*, concentrated on the city itself with just a glimpse of its neighbours. That, however, left quite a number of shots unused that I either didn't have space for or were simply not pictures of Portsmouth. This second book, therefore, uses all but a few of Jim's remaining photographs, and like the first, compares them to shots I've taken over the past 33 years.

On our aerial tour, we will be flying in a helicopter at around 1,000ft, to take a look at many of the towns and villages in the Portsmouth area, as well as flying over the city itself. On the way, I have tried to identify at least some of the buildings we can see that have been lost to time, and remember some of the businesses that used to occupy them.

Jim's early photographs date back to the early 1950s when he flew, with a pilot-friend of his, from Portsmouth Airport. Most were shot in black & white but in the 1960s he started using colour slide film as faster, sharper and more affordable films became available. Despite these improvements they were still rather temperamental, requiring careful temperature storage both before and after processing and had a tendency to fade or discolour with age. Jim's slides were no exception but, with the help of modern imaging editing software, I have attempted to restore some of their original quality.

We start this aerial tour at Havant, a town that has seen many changes in the 33 years I've been flying, and a town I covered on my first ever aerial photographic commission.

Compare these two photographs, from 1988 and 2019 respectively. In the middle we can see West Street Arcade, I'm sure many people will remember Toojays toy shop. The area from North Street to the bus station, including the arcade, was redeveloped as The Meridian Centre which opened in 1991. We can also see the new developments of Solent Retail Park on Solent Road, and Central Retail Park on what was Potash Terrace, still visible in the earlier shot. There are now plans to redevelop the area south of Havant train station, including Market Parade, North Street and West Street with retail, residential apartments and commercial properties.

Havant

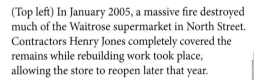

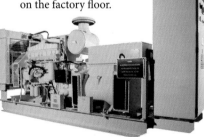

(Top left) In January 2005, a massive fire destroyed much of the Waitrose supermarket in North Street. Contractors Henry Jones completely covered the remains while rebuilding work took place, allowing the store to reopen later that year.

(Above) This is the Tesco store on Solent Road with the distinctive wavy roof in 2005. It was replaced in 2009 by the larger store we see today on the adjacent page.

Generator photographed on the factory floor.

(Above) This 1987 shot of Solent Road and Brockhampton Lane, shows it was a largely industrial area comprising mainly factories, including generator manufacturer Dawson Keith in the centre.

(Right) This is the same area in 2017, and it's now barely recognisable. Most of the factories have been replaced by the large retail units of Solent Retail Park including; Hobbycraft, Halfords, Sports Direct and a huge M&S. The Tesco store is clearly much larger than its wavy roofed predecessor, and Bosmere Medical Centre has been built on the former playing field.

Here in 1987, on the south side of the A27, was one of two IBM manufacturing plants in the UK. It was known within the computing industry for producing disc files for PCs and flexi-circuits. The IBM Havant plant closed in 1991, the site now forming part of Langstone Technology Park which contains dozens of technology companies. Southmoor Lane has been extended to accommodate the new industrial areas built on the fields to the south. In the distance (top-left of the photograph), you can see the road and rail bridges to Hayling Island, which is where we are heading to next.

This photo taken by Jim in the early 1950s shows the original wooden Langstone toll bridge to Hayling Island. There was a weight limit that required some bus passengers to get out and walk across if there were too many on board. In 1956, this was replaced by the concrete bridge which is still in use today, although the toll wasn't lifted until 1960. We can also see the timber swing bridge, with an operator's cabin, that would carry the Hayling Billy on the Hayling branch line. By 1962 this bridge also needed replacing but British Railways decided it should close, due to the unreasonably large investment required. Consequently, the final trains ran on 2nd November 1963.

Oysters were farmed on the Hayling Island Oyster Beds from as early as 1819, and indeed up until the 1970s. In 1996, the oyster beds were restored by Havant Borough Council, creating a wildlife haven, and the area renamed West Hayling Local Nature Reserve. Here they are in 2001, when they had become an important seabird breeding site for Little Terns, Common Terns, Black Headed and Mediterranean Gulls and Ring Plovers.

Hayling Island

(Left) Looking south from North Hayling in 2003.

(Above) The Hayling Branch Line terminated at West Town station; all that remained here in 1987 was this derelict former goods shed. In 1992 Hayling Island Dramatic Society, combined with huge local support and a grant from Hampshire County Council, raised sufficient funds to start Phase 1 of its refurbishment and conversion into a 144-seat theatre. Generous contributions from local businesses, further fundraising and a lottery grant, all helped complete the building work.

We now cross Langstone Harbour to take a look around Portsmouth.
(Above) A dramatic early morning shot of sea fog coming through the entrance to Langstone Harbour.
(Right) Low tide at Langstone Harbour near Great Salterns Quay, now removed, in 1999.

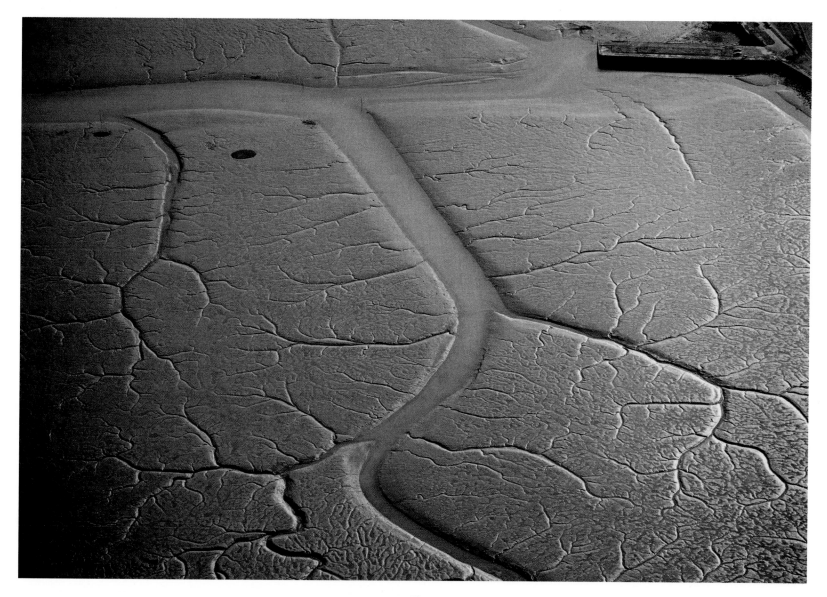

Portsmouth

We're now over Portsea Island to look at Baffins, Copnor and Hilsea.

(Right) In this late 1960s view over Baffins and Milton, we can see the allotments that were to become Tangier Park and Milton Lake being in-filled with domestic refuse and other waste to become Milton Common. This was also before the housing estates around Moorings Way were built.

(Below) G.A. Day Ltd. in Burrfields Road, seen here in 1987, was a family-run builder's merchants with its roots in Portsmouth. It expanded in the '90s, opening stores across the south, but was taken over by Grafton Group in 2001, becoming part of Buildbase.

(Below right) Looking south-west over Chichester Road in the 1960s, it's interesting to see the majority of houses still have their original slate roofs. The grand buildings in the top right-hand corner are Meredith Infant and Isambard Brunel Junior Schools.

Hilsea

(Right) London Road runs across this shot with The Green Posts in the centre, a well-known landmark pub in Hilsea. It is at this point, on the opposite side of the road, there is an obelisk marking the boundary of the Borough of Portsmouth that was erected in 1799.

(Below) While Jim was up taking his photographs he often went past his school, which of course is less than a mile away from Portsmouth Airport where he would fly from. Here are two shots, probably taken on the same flight in 1962.

Tipner

Here, looking northwest over Tipner in the late 1950s, we can see Tipner Range, with Portchester Castle and Horsea Island in the distance. The circle on the grass in the centre was actually the site of Stamshaw Swimming Pool. Work to build 52 maisonettes and 51 garages on part of this site started in 1962, the rest is now known as Tipner Green.

The M275 now carves its way through Tipner, shortening the shooting range by 200 yards and bisecting Harry Pounds scrapyard. Here in 2013, work was underway to provide a 'park-and-ride' service to the city. The remains of the dog track can be seen in the bottom right corner.

The entire Tipner Range area is soon to be completely redeveloped in a massive project known as Tipner West. The 140-acre site is to be transformed into a 'marine employment campus' with R&D facilities and makerspaces, and over 4,000 homes, but no roads. Work is expected to start in 2023. Meanwhile, we can compare it before and after the M275 motorway, in 1969 and 2011 respectively.

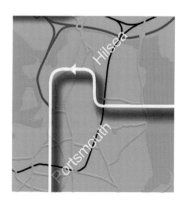

We now head south over Stamshaw and on to the city centre.

(Above) This is another shot of Jim's taken in the late 1960s. This is where Twyford Avenue and Stamshaw Road part company by The Beresford pub, taken at the time the new one-way road system had just been introduced.

(Right) The Beresford has now been converted into houses and can be seen at the bottom right of this view towards Kingston Crescent and Kingston Road. Built in 1983, the large flat-roofed building on the left of this shot, started life as a Presto food market. It was later taken over by Somerfield and subsequently became a Co-Op in 2009. The building was vacant during 2016 and was being refurbished for Lidl when this was taken in 2017.

This is All Saints Church and Commercial Road c.1970, with the recently completed tower blocks, Pickwick, Barkis and Nickleby Houses and other maisonettes that were built to replace the bombed terraced housing that once filled the area. What remains of this part of Commercial Road, seen in the bottom left of this shot, is now known as Old Commercial Road. To the right is the ABC Cinema and The Royal Hospital, and opposite is Beaumonts outfitters and The Royal pub.

(Right) As we move down Commercial Road we can't miss the Tricorn Centre, which for me had to be the best car park ever made, with its numerous levels and spiral ramps. This shot was taken shortly before its demise in 2004, but on demolition day, protestors hoping to 'Save the Tricorn', momentarily delayed the start of its destruction.

Further down Commercial Road we find its junction with Arundel Street and Edinburgh Road in these two very similar shots. Running across the top of Jim's 1970 view is the dockyard branch line. One of the level crossing gates has been preserved and is still in position on Edinburgh Road.

(Right) Zurich House wasn't built until 1973 with its distinctive shape following the curve of the old railway line. It has now been converted into student accommodation, had an extension built to one side, and been renamed Catherine House. While to the right, as we see it here in 2018, there is a Travelodge Hotel under construction. The half-built tower in the centre and the tall building nearing completion in the foreground are also both student accommodation blocks, an indication of how Portsmouth University has come to dominate the city centre.

Today, tower blocks seem to be springing up all over the city centre, but that is nothing new. This shot of Jim's, overlooking the city in 1970, has Sarah Robinson House on Queen Street in the foreground, a 21-storey residential tower block completed in 1967, and the numerous high-rise towers of Somerstown. In the centre is Portsmouth and Southsea Station and Victoria Park.

(Right) This is another shot with Portsmouth and Southsea Station in the centre, now in 2018, it is surrounded by student accommodation blocks, a hotel and the civic offices.

This is Somerstown in 1972 with the new tower blocks of Ladywood, Handsworth and Edgbaston Houses in the foreground. This shot clearly shows the paths of the roads that were once densely packed with terraced houses. In the centre of the shot, we can see Cumberland, Carlisle, Froddington and Abingdon Roads, all these were cleared in the 1980s to make way for Winston Churchill Avenue and Holbrook Road. In the background is Fratton goods yard and, barely distinguishable, Fratton Park before the stands were built.

The Somerstown Community Hub and council offices bridge Winston Churchill Avenue as it passes between the towers. It was close to completion here in this 2014 photo.

We're towards the end of Commercial Road now, or as it was in 1968, in another of Jim's colour slides. It shows two more tower blocks, Leamington House and Horatia House that were completed in 1965. The cleared site towards the top of the shot is where Victoria Barracks stood. All that remains of the barracks is now The City Museum and Art Gallery, and Alexandra Road was renamed Museum Road to reflect that. The rest of the site is now Pembroke Park housing estate and a hotel.

Opposite the museum was Portsmouth University's Ravelin Car Park. At the time of writing it was being redeveloped as a major indoor sports facility that will include a sports hall and swimming pool. In 2018, before construction could commence, an exploratory archaeological dig revealed some of Portsmouth's historic fortifications that protected the naval port in the 17th century.

Next page) As we move towards Southsea we can look back at the city centre in 1972 compared to 2019.

This 1958 slide is, sadly, really showing its age, but I thought I'd include it as it does show something I thought was rather interesting. The Southsea branch line is always a fascinating subject and there are maps available online that show its route from Fratton Station to East Southsea Station. Although long gone, some evidence of its existence still remains today. Its distinctive curved route can be followed from the top left of Jim's photo, along Heidelberg Road and through the area of cleared land on St Ronans Road and Parkstone Avenue. This area would shortly be developed for housing. The station site itself has already been redeveloped although the terminus building facing Granada Road was being used as a garage at this time and wasn't demolished until the 1970s. Chewter Close, a cul-de-sac of houses was built in its place, they can be found in the top left corner of my 2019 photo, alongside St Simons Church. South Parade Pier has undergone some major renovations by the new owners after being closed in 2012 due to safety concerns. It now looks magnificent and has seen the return of fairground rides, arcades, shops, restaurants and events.

Southsea

(Left) In 1969, after a refit in Portsmouth Dockyard and with commanding officer Captain J.A. Templeton-Cotill at the helm, HMS *Bulwark* sailed for the Mediterranean Sea to take part in exercises Grecian Vase and Olympic Express, with visits to Gibraltar, Malta, Cyprus, Salonica, Venice, Villefranche-sur-Mer, and Toulon. Shipping movements at the harbour entrance have always attracted interest from members of the crew's family and the general public alike. Jim was obviously pleased to catch Bulwark leaving port, enough to shoot it in both black & white and colour.

(Right) Crowds line the Hot Walls to welcome HMS *Newcastle*'s return to port in 1999, after escorting the aircraft carrier HMS *Invincible* during the Kosovo War.

HMS *Newcastle* was a batch 1 Type 42 destroyer, launched in 1975. After a long service, it was announced in July 2004 – as part of the *Delivering Security in a Changing World* review – that *Newcastle* would be decommissioned the following January and placed into inactive reserve. Whilst sitting out at Fareham Creek she was cannibalised heavily in order to keep the remaining Type 42 destroyers operational. In 2008 she left Portsmouth for the last time, headed for Aliağa, Turkey, to be scrapped.

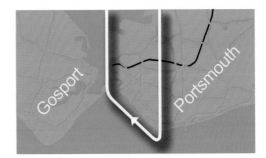

We now travel through the harbour entrance
to see the dockyard and ferry port.

Jim's view over HMS *Vernon* and Portsmouth Harbour Station also covers a large part of the dockyard and upper reaches of the harbour in the early 1970s.

HMS *Vernon* is in the foreground of this 1969 slide of Portsea from Jim. Queen Street runs up the left side where there is evidence of a lot of construction work in progress. The large playing field on the right was the United Services Recreation Ground, it now includes a running track and is known as HMS *Temeraire*.

Portsmouth had three Director Class paddle tugs; RMAS Tug *Forceful*, *Griper* and *Grinder* that entered service in the late 1950s as they were ideal for manoeuvring aircraft carriers around the dockyard. One can be seen in the foreground of Jim's slide and may well be the one we saw following *Bulwark* out of the harbour earlier. After 20-years of service, *Griper* and *Grinder* were sold to Harry Pounds for scrap. *Forceful* was transferred to Directorate of Naval Air Warfare (DNAW) for use as a missile target at Aberporth Range and, despite several attempts to rescue and preserve her, in 1990 she returned to Cairnryan to be broken up.

These two shots of the dockyard were taken on the same day in June 1956, where we can see some very notable ships. In the centre is, of course, HMS *Victory*, a 104-gun first-rate ship of the line and flagship of the First Sea Lord, the oldest naval ship still in commission in the world and now a museum ship. Berthed on Victory Jetty is HMY *Britannia* when she would have been only 3-years old. Battleship USS *Iowa* (BB-61) is alongside the South Railway Jetty during a brief visit on a midshipman's cruise. It, too, is now a museum ship and is moored at San Pedro, Los Angeles, California.

Also visible, through the smoke from the power station, is the Victoria branch line, a viaduct built in 1876 to bring Queen Victoria directly into the dockyard to board the royal yacht. The last royal train to use it carried King George VI and Queen Elizabeth, when they departed for Canada and the U.S.A. in 1939. A swing bridge, at the end nearest the dockyard, was damaged during the war and removed in 1946, although the rest wasn't demolished until 1962.

(Right) This is HMS *Queen Elizabeth* on the renamed Princess Royal Jetty, in 2018. The jetty has been upgraded and strengthened to support the 65,000 tonne Queen Elizabeth-class aircraft carriers and was officially opened by HRH Princess Anne in March 2017. In No.2 Basin, in the foreground, are minesweepers HMS *Hurworth* and HMS *Cattistock*.

Tall ships from around the world gathered for the *Cutty Sark* Tall Ships' Race in Portsmouth Harbour on 15th-18th August 2002.
Amongst them was this magnificent ship, *Sedov*, the largest sailing ship in the world, built in 1920 in Germany but now under
a Russian flag. Originally she would carry nitrate from Chile and grain from Australia, but she is now a cadet training ship.

(Top left) Chalk can be seen here being used to expand Mill Wharf into Fountain Lake in 1958. This extension was for handling ballast, aggregates and fuel oil.

(Above) In Jim's late '60s slide of Fountain Lake, there appears to be the signs of further expansion to the quays in what was to become the ferry port.

(Left) In the foreground is HMS *Centaur*; she was launched in 1947 but delays due to the end of the war meant she was not commissioned until 1953. She was originally built with an axial flight deck but this was modified in Portsmouth to an angled deck very soon after. Here in the late 1960s, she was used for the accommodation of crews from *Hermes* and *Bulwark* during their refits, before being scrapped in 1972.

Portsmouth International Port now has five berths, all in operation here in 2013, viewed clockwise from the left:

Brittany Ferries, *Normandie Express* – introduced in 2005, she provides a fast ferry crossing to Cherbourg and Caen.

Swan Hellenic, *Minerva* – Canadian tour operator G Adventures bought the British cruise brand Swan Hellenic and operated the small cruise ship until the All Leisure Group company was declared insolvent.

MV *Bretagne* – ordered by Brittany Ferries in the late 1980s, she was one of the first true cruise-ferries, offering cruise-type facilities on a ferry route.

MV *Normandie* – also operated by Brittany Ferries, she was built at Kværner Masa-Yards, Turku, Finland, and has been sailing for them since 1992.

MS *Commodore Clipper* – a 'Ro-Ro' passenger vessel operated by the Guernsey-based company Condor Ferries. The ship has a maximum capacity of 500 passengers and 350 cars or 92 lorries/12m trailers. The vessel was launched in 1999 and currently operates on the Portsmouth to Channel Islands route.

Moored at Whale Island is HMS *Bristol*. This was the only Type 82 destroyer ever built for the Royal Navy, designed to defend a class of aircraft carrier that was never actually built.

Gosport

(Left) As we cross over the upper reaches of Portsmouth Harbour, we find quite a variety of vessels in the 'mothball fleet' on the reserve moorings, or trot.

On the western side of the harbour we arrive at Hardway and can make an interesting comparison between these two photos.

(Below left) In Jim's photo from 1969, there are more ships in 'operational reserve' including the large depot ship HMS *Tyne*, which at this time was being used as a harbour accommodation ship. Moored at Vosper's pier is the Hovermarine prototype hovercraft VT1, which was built at their factory in Portchester. In the foreground is Greens Bakery and the Vosper's works, while in the distance is Priddy's Hard pier.

(Below) In my photo from 2000, clearance of the old factories is complete and work on the new housing estate is well underway.

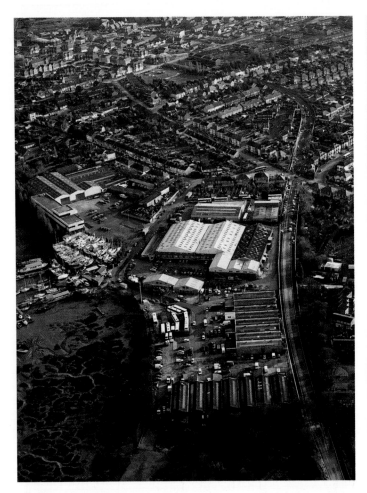

Under construction in 2002, and slicing through Hardway, is the Priddy's Hard link road. It is now officially named Heritage Way, and allows easy access to the massive housing development to the south.

Work had only just begun on the link road when this was taken in 2000 and shows where it will join the A32. This corner is where the Brockhurst Gate retail park has now been built.

Also to be found here is the spectacular Fort Brockhurst, with its moat and circular moated keep. Fort Brockhurst was one of a chain of five similar forts known as the Gosport Advanced Line, built to protect Portsmouth Harbour from a potential land-based attack. Seen here in 2009, the fort is only accessible during Heritage Open Days.

Moving on down from Hardway are the remains of the 18th century fortifications of Priddy's Hard Fort. It is surrounded by ramparts that were completed in 1757 and can still be seen today. Much of the area has been redeveloped for housing but some of the older buildings have been retained and are now home to Explosion! Museum of Naval Firepower. Other parts, such as the cordite magazine, remain unused and overgrown here in 2011. For many years, Priddy's Hard was part of Royal Naval Armaments Depot (RNAD), Gosport, supplying ordnance and training to Commonwealth and foreign countries. Its last significant activity was during the Falklands Conflict in 1982. In the background, crossing Forton Lake, is the Millennium Bridge, part of the Gosport Waterfront Trail. It features an opening span to allow taller vessels to pass into Portsmouth Harbour.

The former Forton Lake bridge is in the background of this 1998 shot. It too has a gap but no way of closing it and looks very dilapidated.

(Far right) This leads us to the Royal Clarence Victuallers Yard, which once housed a rum store, a granary, a bakery and a slaughterhouse. Originally there was talk of the slaughterhouse being converted into a pub, where you would go to get 'slaughtered' so-to-speak. In the event it was converted into a gym, so, much the same then! Many of these buildings are Grade II listed and, as we can see from my shot of 2011, have been sympathetically restored for a mixture of residential, commercial and leisure uses.

Camper and Nicholsons is a name that has long been associated with Gosport, here at Gosport Marina. The company was created when Ben Nicholson partnered William Camper in 1855, who had been building small trading boats there since 1820. They went on to design and manufacture some of the world's finest racing yachts, including the famous J-class. This is how it looked in 1987.

The Gosport yard went through some difficult times and changes of ownership in the early 2000s but locally based company Marina Projects took over management of the site, letting out the workshops to numerous marine-related businesses and it became Endeavour Quay. This 2013 shot was taken just before the property was taken over by Premier Marinas Ltd.

(Right) Mumby Road curves around the impressive, colonial-style St George Barracks, the southern part seen here in 2000. After being closed for nearly 10 years, the Grade II listed buildings were soon to be redeveloped into residential apartments in a gated estate.

The tower blocks of Harbour and Seward Towers dominate the skyline of Gosport waterfront, commanding spectacular views over the harbour entrance. Coming towards the camera in the centre of this shot is the South Street dual carriageway, When this was taken in 1970, we can see it coming to a halt where it meets Walpole Park. In the foreground we see The Anchorage housing estate under construction and the area near the gasholder is now an Asda supermarket. On the right is the tall, exposed, wooden pedestrian bridge over Haslar Lake, known locally as 'Pneumonia Bridge'. The lifting section of the earlier bridge had been damaged beyond repair so it was extended upward to allow gunboats headed for HMS *Hornet* to pass underneath.

(Right) 'Pneumonia Bridge' was replaced in 1980 with a single lane concrete bridge, seen here on a lovely, clear, summer's day in July 2013, with views all the way to Hayling Island. Haslar Marina car park is built on land reclaimed from Haslar Lake. The pond in the centre is part of the system of moats and defences that once surrounded Gosport, dating back to the Napoleonic Wars.

At the tip of the Gosport peninsula stood Fort Blockhouse, bought by the Admiralty at the beginning of the 20th century to set up HMS *Dolphin*, Britain's first submarine base. A number of A-Class submarines can be seen on the jetties in Jim's photo from 1970. Also clearly visible is the diving tank, or more correctly, the Submarine Escape Training Tank (SETT). It was commissioned in 1954, with the first students trained in July of that year. The Royal Navy discontinued pressurised submarine escape training in March 2009 but it was still used for non-pressurised drills until the facilities were moved to Scotland in 2020. The tower itself remains today, and is a listed building.

(Right) This is the same view in 2010, and there is still a submarine to see. This one is HMS *Alliance*, the only Second World War-era submarine remaining, and it is open to explore at the Royal Navy Submarine Museum. Within the museum there are others on display, including HMS *Holland I* and HMS *X24*.

Haslar

When completed in 1762, the Royal Naval Hospital Haslar was the largest brick building in Europe. With accommodation for over 2,000 sailors, it provided the most up-to-date treatments available at the time. In 2001 it went into partnership with Portsmouth Hospitals NHS Trust but just 6-years later, it ceased to be an MOD-managed hospital and 254 years of medical care to the armed forces came to an end. In 2009, it finally closed completely.

The site has been sold to private developers and planning consent has been granted for a major redevelopment scheme which will see the site used largely for continuing care purposes. Due to the large amount of floor space, there will also be a range of complementary facilities including residential homes, a care home, retirement units, offices and business premises, a health centre, a hotel, tearooms, a restaurant/bar and a convenience store, along with a church, public hall and heritage centre.

(Above left) Jim's 1950s photo.

(Above) 2019, clearance of later additional buildings has started.

(Right) 2010, closed prior to any demolition work.

(Left) As we follow Stoke Lake we arrive at Alverstoke where the L.& S.W.R. Stokes Bay branch line crosses a viaduct on its way to the 600 feet long Stokes Bay Pier. There was once a ferry service to Ryde on the Isle of Wight operating from the pier; in 1863 it would have cost you 1s 6d for a 1st class return crossing that took just 15 minutes. After the First World War, it was acquired by the Admiralty and was put to a variety of uses including preparation and testing of torpedoes. This shot, however, shows it shortly before it was dismantled. Work started in 1972 but it wasn't until 1987 that the pile bases were removed completely, being a hazard to shipping. In the foreground is 'The Park', a public recreation ground since 1887 when it was bought from the Gosport and Alverstoke Board for £100 from the Church of England. The circular feature, known as The Dell, is probably a former gravel pit but now makes an ideal stadium and is marked out as a rugby pitch with floodlighting.

(Above) The area known as Angleseyville was developed by Robert Cruikshank, and named in honour of the Marquis of Anglesey. The speculator building known as 'The Crescent' and the Anglesea Arms Hotel were completed in 1830, emulating the Georgian crescents of the day, but these were only the first parts of what was intended to be an even grander development. Sadly, it wasn't a financial success so the rest was never built but what we see here in 2019 is Grade II listed.

(Above) Fort Gilkicker is a post-Palmerston Fort forming part of the historic fortifications along the south coast. Constructed in brick, it is semi-circular with 22 casemates and continued to be used until 1956 when the coastal defence system was abolished. Plans to convert the Fort for residential use have recently been approved.

(Above right) Moving west along the coast we arrive at Lee-on-the-Solent High Street and Marine Parade with its independent shops and charming seaside cafés. Much of the architecture in the area is of the Art Deco style; here and amongst the nearby houses, there are some very fine examples.

(Right) The airfield at Lee grew out of the Fleet Air Arm seaplane base, Royal Naval Air Station Lee-on-the-Solent (HMS *Daedalus*). The hangers and slipway for the seaplanes were built in 1918 and can still be seen today. The airfield at Lee has an incredibly long and eventful history, between 1939 and 1945 some 81 squadrons operating 21 types of aircraft were based here. Later, in 1962, the slipway and hangers were put to use by the Joint Service Hovercraft Trials Unit. The Hovercraft Museum now occupies one of these sheds and offers trips around the Solent on open days. In my 2006 shot, there are two SRN4 cross channel hovercraft, *Princess Anne* and *Princess Margaret*. Sadly, the latter has now been broken up.

Lee-on-the-Solent

This 2017 overview of Lee-on-the-Solent shows the Cherque Farm residential development of 1,063 homes to the east of the seaside town. The new road linking Broom Way to Privett Road has created a new boundary with Alver Valley and in the middle distance is the renamed Solent Airport.

Hill Head and Titchfield

(Left) As we fly westward past the airfield along the coast, we approach Stubbington and Hill Head in the late 1960s.

(Below left) When shooting from a high-wing aeroplane, there is always the risk of a wheel or wing strut encroaching into the field-of-view. I've deliberately not cropped the wing strut off this image or it would've also cut off Seafield Park, a former prep school that became a Fleet Air Arm base in 1955, housing the Air Medical School, Safety Equipment & Training School, Central Air Medical Board, Naval Aircrew Advisory Board and Naval Aircraft and Marine Examination Board. This site is now a housing estate with roads named after various aircraft carriers.

(Right) The River Meon meanders its way through the wetlands of the nature reserve at Titchfield Haven. This view was taken in 2014 after significant rainfall although water levels are managed to provide the ideal conditions for wildfowl and migrating birds.

(Far right) Following the River Meon upstream, we arrive at Titchfield in 1999. The river was once navigable to this point and Titchfield had a busy port. St Peter's Church, centre right, was established in 680, some of the original structure still survives, making it one of the oldest churches in the country.

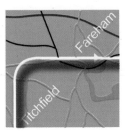

Further upstream we find the ruins of Place House & Abbey of St Mary & St John the Evangelist, better known as Titchfield Abbey. What we see today is a deliberately created 'romantic ruin' and is often used as a backdrop for wedding photoshoots, such as the one here in September 2012. Prior to this, it was occupied by the Delmé family who, in turn, had bought it from Thomas Wriothesley, the Earl of Southampton. It was Henry VIII in the 16th century who dissolved the abbey that had been founded in 1222.

We now turn east towards Fareham, flying over Furzehall Farm and an area once known for its brickworks, potteries and tobacco pipe manufacture. Wickham Road leads us past the Kiln Acre industrial estate and Potteries business centre with names that reflect its past. The building work underway here in 2012 is a new housing estate on the former site of St Christopher's Hospital. Before joining the National Health Service in 1948, St Christopher's was a Public Assistance Institution, but prior to 1930, it was the Fareham Union Workhouse.

Fareham

Here are three views of the Old Turnpike, Broadcut, and Wallington area.

(Far left) In the centre of Jim's 1969 photo is Turnpike Garage. Look closely and you can see there are still four petrol pumps on the forecourt but, in 1970, they stopped selling petrol and became Turnpike Tyres. At the bottom of the shot is a campsite where Wickham Road Roundabout now lies. To the right, the caravan site has been replaced by the supermarket's petrol station, and the area of Nissen huts is where the J. Sainsbury store was built.

(Above left) My 1995 shot shows the original J. Sainsbury brick building that was fashionable at the time for out-of-town retail parks. In front of the store, facing Broadcut itself, there is a small factory building and six properties known as Riverside Terrace. The road down from Fareham town was called Wallington Hill, a road that was largely replaced by the pedestrian bridge over the dual carriageway, Wallington Way. Local opposition prevented the original 1715 Wallington Bridge from being removed when the dual carriageway was built in the late 70s. As such, it still obstructs the flow of the River Wallington causing it to occasionally flood.

(Below left) By 2011, J. Sainsbury was known simply as Sainsbury's, and the building refurbished with modern white cladding. The petrol filling station has grown and now includes a convenience store. The factory building and cottages have been replaced by two retail units which, over the years, have been occupied by retailers Dreams, Poundstretcher, Staples, and at the time of writing, PureGym.

Crossing the viaduct here at Quay Street Roundabout in 1998, is a special mainline steam tour being pulled by a Merchant Navy Class 4-6-2 locomotive, number 35028 *Clan Line*. The former foundry site is clearly visible, soon to be redeveloped as a Tesco supermarket, the roof of which can be seen in my 2013 shot. (Right)

(Right) Arriving in Portchester, at the Cornaway Lane roundabout, we find The Seagull. This pub has been altered and extended many times, both before and after this 1998 shot. It is now part of the Hungry Horse restaurant/pub chain.

(Below) Jim often took shots of schools or houses for his fellow teachers, like this one from the 1950s of the north-west corner of the roundabout. These long back gardens have all since been redeveloped with the houses of Rockingham Way, and the fields at the top are now part of Portchester Crematorium.

(Lower right) In 2012, residents of Portchester were provided with a brand new community centre, which accommodates a wide range of community activities, from childcare to beer festivals. This replaced the very rundown, out of date, dangerous, and soon to be demolished building that we can also see here.

(Far right) In 1956 Portchester was growing rapidly, we can see the houses of The Queensway and The Close under construction in the foreground. Near the top of this shot are the white buildings of Warings Cement works, where they manufactured paving slabs. It is now Castle Shore Park but still referred to locally as Warings Field.

We'll now go on a quick orbit around Portchester with another 1956 photo from Jim. In the foreground is Cranleigh Road leading to Wicor School, which is being redeveloped as the Heritage Gardens housing estate in my shot from 1999 (Right). Wicor Mill was demolished c.1935 but materials from it were used to construct the chimney for a factory, centre right in Jim's shot, which made glue from animal bones. This process created a rather unpleasant smell known locally as the 'Portchester Pong'. Portchester has retained some of its green space but one must wonder for how much longer, some of what we see here in my 20-year-old photo has already gone.

A tour of Portchester wouldn't be complete without a look at Portchester Castle, looking as stunning as ever in Jim's late 1960s slide and my low-level shot from 2008.

(Right) Here's the village on market day in 2014. At this time, Lidl were campaigning for public support to build a store on a derelict pine furniture factory site on the Castle Trading Estate. Fareham Council wanted them to build it on the south car park so Lidl, who already owned the factory site, launched another campaign to 'Save Our Car Park'. The campaigns were successful, Lidl got their store on Castle Trading Estate but the victim and main opponent to the new store was the Co-op supermarket, which closed a few years later.

North Harbour

Here are three stages of the redevelopment of Northarbour. The first 1999 shot shows the Tesco store and Compass Road office development, the first buildings on the reclaimed land behind the Southampton Road houses. Noticeable too is the notorious Johnson & Johnson roundabout, named after the Johnson & Johnson factory, which runs alongside.

Moving on to 2002 and the decks, so-to-speak, have been cleared. All but four of the Southampton Road houses have been demolished, as has the Johnson & Johnson factory. There are more offices on Compass Road, including a nursery school and a Land Rover dealership. Tesco also sees some expansion in progress, along with rearrangement of the car park to make up for lost capacity.

By 2018 only two of the houses remain, the other two made way for a McDonalds, and almost all the vacant plots have been filled. The Pall Corporation offices, formerly Raymarine, occupy the Johnson & Johnson site, plus some land gained when the junction was redesigned as crossroads.

Cosham and Drayton

(Far left) This is Northern Road, Cosham High Street and London Road as it starts to climb Portsdown Hill in 2012. We'll follow the A3 in a moment but first we look down Havant Road and Knowsley Road.

(Left) Moving east on Havant Road, across the bottom of this late 1960s slide, we come to St Colman's Church. At the very top, the exposed chalk of Portsdown Hill shows work on the construction of Portsdown Park had started.

(Below left) Going east along Knowsley Road will take you to Old Manor Way and Kinross Crescent, in another of Jim's slides from around the same time.

(Below) While he was up flying, Jim made a point of photographing many of the schools in the area. This is Manor Court School in the 1960s, a school that has retained its extensive playing fields to this day.

Widley and Purbrook

Following the A3 north we go up and over Portsdown Hill to Widley and find the recently built houses in The Dale. London Road just cuts across the top right-hand corner and Portsdown Hill Road is in the top left of these two photos taken by Jim. The colour slide was taken in the late 1960s but the black & white shot shows the scene slightly earlier, in the '50s. Near the bottom of this shot is Purbrook Park School, built around a magnificent house by John Deverell in 1839 but extended significantly around this time to cope with rising student numbers.

(Right) Expanding too is Purbrook, with building well underway of this new residential estate in 2017. Oak Vale is only one phase of the development of Newlands Farm, phase 2 is already planned to the north and we'll see yet more house building when we get to Waterlooville.

Waterlooville

In 1998 this recently completed MFI superstore opened on the site of the former Broadlands Mansion Hotel. The hotel and grounds became a garden centre in the '60s before being demolished to make way for the retail shed now in its place. The building is currently occupied by builder's merchants Wickes and Topps Tiles.

The eastern side of Waterlooville town centre was redeveloped in 2000, with a new Waitrose supermarket, a parade of smaller shop units, a Wilko and additional car parking. We've seen many schools in Jim's photos so I'm sure he'll be pleased that I caught Waterloo School in the middle of this one.

(Far right) While Purbrook spreads north, Waterlooville is spreading south just as quickly. Brambles Business Park was once a farm amidst the Forest of Bere, but the land was turned over to industrial use and by the 1980s the office and industrial estate really took off. The site of the original farm buildings became GEC Marconi offices, developing guidance systems for the Spearfish torpedo, and can be seen here being demolished in 2014. The site has since been redeveloped again: 2017 saw the building of a Lidl supermarket on the same spot.

The recent development around Brambles Farm, to the south of Hambledon Road, has been largely residential with new developments such as Berewood, Old Park Farm and Wellington Park. To cater for the increase in population to the area, new retail units have been incorporated, as well as a recycling centre, a care home and, on the edge of the current development, a new primary school.

These three views, of the western end of the development, were taken from roughly the same position in 2001, 2013 and 2016. They show how the business park expanded and how the residential housing is now spreading over the former farmland.

(Left) This overview from the eastern end was taken in 2016.

(Below left) Berewood Primary School in 2014.

(Below) The Berewood Estate in 2017.

For Sale board featuring one of my
aerial photos of the site.

Moving back along Hambledon Road towards Waterlooville in 1987, we find Payless DIY and Courts Mammoth Superstore. They were the first two occupants of the newly built Wellington Retail Park; other retailers to occupy these buildings were Sofas and Rooms and DFS. In the background are the workshops and garages of Wadham Stringer. The Wadham family have a long history with Waterlooville, dating back to 1871 when they were in the drapery business, but it was brothers John Harold and Wilfred Charles Wadham that established the motor trade connection in 1905 with Wadham Bros. In 1963, the company moved into the factory we can see in the top left of this shot, where they made buses, coaches and ambulances. Wadham Bros amalgamated with Stringer Motors in 1968 and it became Wadham Stringer (Coachbuilders) Ltd. To the right is their Wadham Stringer car dealership business, selling Jaguar, Land Rover and Austin Rover cars. The company was bought and sold a number of times in the 1990s, manufacturing ceased in 2009, and the site finally sold in 2014.

Wadham Stringer (Coachbuilders) Ltd. MIAB
(Modular Interchangeable Ambulance Body)
manufactured in Waterlooville.

(Left) Here we see it in 2017, with the Wadham Stringer factory replaced by a Sainsbury's store, and the showroom and offices replaced by more retail units. Even the original Wellington retail park buildings have been redeveloped and there is the addition of a new slip-road into the car parks to create access from the roundabout.

We're now back at the top of the town centre where we can see The Heroes pub in 2018, near the junction with Hulbert Road. The history of this pub, or at least its name, goes back to the dawn of the town itself. Originally, The Heroes of Waterloo was a coaching inn on the intersection of the Hambledon to Stakes Hill and London to Portsmouth roads, built around the time of the battle of Waterloo.

Jim also took a shot of Hulbert Road and the new houses in Warfield Avenue and Warfield Crescent where, in the 1950s, many of the properties were yet to be built.

Cowplain

Travelling further north up the A3 we reach Cowplain and one of the last remaining significant areas of the Royal Forest of Bere, the Queen's Inclosure. Most likely named after Queen Victoria, the 100-acres of ancient woodland are home to 200-year-old sessile oaks and a variety of wildlife.

(Left) This turning to the left, off London Road and opposite the Queen's Inclosure, is Queen's Road. One of a couple of shots Jim took here in 1967.

(Below left) In the centre of this shot is Firs Avenue, with more housing under construction alongside Cowplain School on Hart Plain Avenue. These are on the site of Oakmont, a mansion house whose land was sold off in various lots and parcels in the 1950s and '60s. The house can still be seen in this photo, but it was finally demolished in 1968. In the foreground there is a terrace of new shops, one of which would've been the food store Pinks around this time. It later became Liptons but the property changed hands many times over the following years. Building of the Waitrose supermarket, that became Lidl, is yet to start as it wasn't to open until 1969.

(Opposite) These four colour slides of Jim's show the extent of house building going on to the north of Waterlooville in the late 1960s and early '70s.

The top left shot is centred on the circular Morley Crescent and Longwood Avenue that leads to Milton Road.

Top right is Kendal Close, off the A3 that runs across the bottom.

Bottom left is an overview of the Hazleton Estate and bottom right, Hazleton Way drops down from the A3 again, clearly showing the newly built road and houses.

The A3(M) has taken much of the through traffic, from Portsmouth to London, away from the A3. Dell Piece West was built to link the two roads at Hazleton Interchange before the two roads merge together a little further north. The resulting triangular piece of land was ripe for development of light industrial and retail units.

(Left) Work started on the Hazleton Interchange industrial estate in 1988, with the removal of topsoil.

(Above) The development of the supermarket followed soon after, seen here in 1999 as Safeway, but in 2004 it was to be acquired by rivals Morrisons.

We are nearing the end of our tour, here, with a view of Horndean in 2006. The village is probably best known for being the home of the award-winning real ale, HSB (Horndean Special Bitter), the flagship brew of George Gale & Co. Ltd. It was at this time 'Gales Ales' were bought by Fullers Brewery for £92 million and beer production was moved to Chiswick, London. The brewery building would later be converted into residential apartments. Initially, Fuller's continued to brew most of the Gale's range of beers but HSB is now the only original brew still available, albeit using a simplified recipe.

(Right) After looking around most of the towns in the area, seeing the relentless development and building work that's taken place over the last 60 years, it's nice to reach the open countryside. We finish our tour with this view over the quintessentially English landscape, with a patchwork of fields in the South Downs National Park, illuminated with dappled light filtered through fluffy cumulus clouds, on a warm summer afternoon.

References and websites

Portsmouth History Centre and Records Office
Portsmouth City Museum
aboutmyarea.co.uk
historicengland.org.uk
historyinportsmouth.co.uk
localhistories.org
maps.nls.uk
navypedia.org
portsmouth.co.uk
portsmouth.gov.uk
publicaccess.portsmouth.gov.uk
skyscrapernews.com
wikipedia.org
20thcenturyfareham.co.uk
thespring.co.uk

With thanks to

Rodney Jones, Bob Daubeney, Lizzie Eacott, Steve Hatton, Colin Cadman, Alistair Plumb
and my friends for their help and encouragement.